**Bird Haiku**

# Bird Haiku

Poems and Illustrations of North American Birds

**SPENCER THOMPSON**

**Oxbow Committee**

Copyright © 2025 by Spencer Thompson.

All rights reserved. With the exception of brief excerpts used in articles and reviews, no part of this work may be reproduced in any form whatsoever without the prior written permission of the publisher.

Design: Cameron Abbas

Oxbow Committee
Sioux Falls, South Dakota
oxbowcommittee.com
spencersodak@gmail.com

First printed in 2025.
ISBN: 979-8-218-62541-2

# Contents

Introduction ............................................................................. 1

A note on haiku as a poetic form ................................................ 2

A note on the art in this book .................................................... 4

Acknowledgments .................................................................... 5

Cooper's hawk ......................................................................... 8

Mourning dove ........................................................................ 10

Downy woodpecker ................................................................. 12

Common nighthawk ................................................................ 14

Common grackle ..................................................................... 16

American crow ........................................................................ 18

Turkey vulture ......................................................................... 20

Red-tailed hawk ...................................................................... 22

Killdeer ................................................................................... 24

Northern harrier ...................................................................... 26

Ring-billed gull ........................................................................ 28

White-faced ibis ...................................................................... 30

Red-winged blackbird .............................................................. 32

American white pelican ........................................................... 34

Mallard ................................................................................... 36

Great horned owl .................................................................... 38

Trumpeter swan ...................................................................... 40

| | |
|---|---:|
| **Canada goose** | 42 |
| **Bufflehead** | 44 |
| **Wood duck** | 46 |
| **Barn swallow** | 48 |
| **Baltimore oriole** | 50 |
| **Yellow-headed blackbird** | 52 |
| **Bald eagle** | 54 |
| **Northern shoveler** | 56 |
| **Cedar waxwing** | 58 |
| **Northern flicker** | 60 |
| **American bittern** | 62 |
| **American woodcock** | 64 |
| **Hooded merganser** | 66 |
| **Green heron** | 68 |
| **Barred owl** | 70 |
| **Great blue heron** | 72 |
| **Wild turkey** | 74 |
| **Yellow warbler** | 76 |
| **Peregrine falcon** | 78 |
| **American barn owl** | 80 |
| **Double-crested cormorant** | 82 |

| | |
|---|---:|
| **Belted kingfisher** | 84 |
| **Canada jay** | 86 |
| **Greater sage-grouse** | 88 |
| **Common loon** | 90 |
| **Western meadowlark** | 92 |
| **Common raven** | 94 |
| **Common merganser** | 96 |
| **American dipper** | 98 |
| **Sandhill crane** | 100 |
| **Snowy egret** | 102 |
| **American robin** | 104 |
| **American kestrel** | 106 |
| **Ruby-throated hummingbird** | 108 |
| **Canvasback** | 110 |
| **Black-capped chickadee** | 112 |
| **Dark-eyed junco** | 114 |
| **Northern cardinal** | 116 |
| **White-breasted nuthatch** | 118 |
| **Red-bellied woodpecker** | 120 |
| **Eastern screech owl** | 122 |
| **Index of artists** | 125 |

# Introduction

These haiku capture meaningful moments within my life that involved a bird in one way or another. The order of the poems in this book is intentional and will take you on a journey—one many birders and outdoor enthusiasts have experienced—from a residential setting, to a car on the road, to a park, to a trail, to a place much further away, and back again.

The images selected for this collection are meant to be companions to the poems, but to varying degrees. There is a traditional art form, *haiga*, that pairs haiku with images, but the approach I used does not follow that style for the most part. Some of the haiku in this book I would simply call "illustrated", as the image depicts the poem's featured bird in a way that is similar to what happened in the haiku. Others are instead just examples of the bird, capturing the likeness of the species and the impression it tends to leave on people. Finally, some pieces of art are essential to the poem and uncover the full meaning of the text.

Life is full of notable moments, and I hope my attempt to capture them resonates with you in some sort of way. Maybe they'll inspire you to go outdoors and start birding—or to write some haiku. Try it out. You might like it.

# A note on haiku as a poetic form

If you're like me, you probably first experienced haiku when you were a child. An elementary school teacher may have told you about the form in a little lesson, and you may have spent some time putting together poems about nature with a 5-7-5 syllable scheme for an assignment. Those lessons were lovely, but they only scratched the surface of what the form is capable of.

I'm not going to attempt to give a thorough history and explanation of the form here. Rather, I just want to give a simple description of what, in my humble opinion, are the key characteristics of a haiku, and how the form is a bit different from what the general public assumes about it.

If you asked a random person what haiku are about, they would most likely say "nature." I don't think that's necessarily a bad answer, but it leaves out some intricacies. For me, the most important element of a haiku is that it captures a slice of time, a moment, in which a scene or a scenario makes an impression on the writer. This moment typically brings about a revelation of some sort through the contrast of two different subjects. Haiku are often set in nature and include subtle seasonal clues about what time of year it is, but neither of those elements are absolute necessities.

Another common characteristic of haiku as a form is that the poet typically tries to remove themselves from the poem so that others can resonate with it. The writer is fully absorbed in the moment they are a part of—and their haiku is an attempt to bring the reader along with them. By removing overly fluffy and poetic terms, haiku poets help readers take in the scene so they can naturally apply their own thoughts, feelings, conclusions and memories to the poem.

As far as the structure of the poem goes, most haiku are indeed three lines, but there are many great haiku that deviate from that number. Furthermore, the 5-7-5 syllable pattern is a bit of a clunky and somewhat forced adaptation of the form for English audiences. The traditional pattern works well in Japanese—for English-language poets, however, it can almost act like a stumbling block to capturing the moment, so I've only used it occasionally in this book. Many scholars have suggested other ways to bring syllabic structure or meter to Western haiku, and I do employ some of their suggestions here, but the primary goal of this book is to capture moments that made an impression on me—not to adhere to strict standards.

Another notable feature of haiku is the portion where the poem "cuts" or "turns", bringing about the resolution or juxtaposition of the poem. In Japanese, this is indicated by a specific kind of word called a *kireji*. To mimic this, English-language poets like myself typically use dashes or some other form of punctuation.

The last note about form I'll make is that haiku has a close relative, *senryū*. Traditionally, these poems follow the same basic structure as haiku, but instead of being about nature, they focus on human interactions and humorous situations. The line between these two forms has become increasingly blurred, so many have just resorted to using the term *haiku* to refer to poems that align with the traits of one or both of these categories.

In this collection, you will find a variety of haiku styles, and you will notice times where I intentionally break rules or implement poetic devices that are not part of the traditional haiku form. My intention in this was not to anger the purists—I did it to more fully express my emotions and adapt the genre to my own personality and preferences.

If haiku interests you and you'd like to learn more about it or find more examples of work, I recommend checking out "The Haiku Handbook" by William J. Higginson. Better yet, try subscribing to a haiku journal or find a book from a small haiku press that sticks out to you. The barrier to entry in this community is low—and the fun to be had is abundant.

# A note on the art in this book

All of the art used in this book is sourced from the public domain. Many of the pieces are scientific illustrations and were primarily used as reference materials in the past. The talented artists and conservationists who created these depictions have contributed immensely to the ornithological community, and I hope this book helps memorialize their work and spread it to generations of birders, poets and art lovers. If it is determined at a later date that a correction or addition needs to be made to the index of artists at the back of the book, I will happily do so.

Quite interestingly, the scientific and common names of some of these birds have changed over time because of taxonomic developments. This makes tracking down early depictions of some species all the more difficult. For the sake of clarity, I have just included the modern names of these birds next to their illustrations.

# Acknowledgments

A special thanks goes out to Cameron Abbas, my collaborator, art curator and layout designer for this collection. Without his help, this book would not exist. Check out his design work at cam-abbas.com and @cam_abbas on Instagram.

I'd also like to thank my wife, children, family, friends and co-workers who have supported and encouraged me along the way. Your contributions have not gone unnoticed.

Of course, above all, I'd like to thank the Lord for all that he has blessed me with. He has truly done great things for me.

# Bird Haiku

**Cooper's hawk**

*Astur cooperii*

Backyard power line,

a Cooper's hawk calling out—

hoarfrost all over

**Mourning dove**

*Zenaida macroura*

Distant dove call

down the old street—

the porch creaks

**Downy woodpecker**

*Dryobates pubescens*

Woodpecker

jabs at the suet—

dark green leaves

**Common nighthawk**

*Chordeiles minor*

My bird app tells me

I have a visitor

I'll never meet

**Common grackle**

*Quiscalus quiscula*

Freshly filled feeder,

the local birds find it

|

|

|

grackles knock it down

**American crow**

*Corvus brachyrhynchos*

Four crows

flying overhead—

I start my car

**Turkey vulture**

*Cathartes aura*

Interstate—

a vulture

cleans a deer

**Red-tailed hawk**

*Buteo jamaicensis*

Sunshine

identifies the hawk's tail—

hunting season

**Killdeer**

*Charadrius vociferus*

Abandoned lot—

the killdeer

in mud

**Northern harrier**

*Circus hudsonius*

Northern harrier

makes low passes

over the field

**Ring-billed gull (top left) and others**

*Larus delawarensis*

The park's parking lot,

full of old fast food litter—

gulls picking through trash

**White-faced ibis**

*Plegadis chihi*

Ibises flying

over the massive reservoir—

scythe-like bills

**Red-winged blackbird**

*Agelaius phoeniceus*

Red wing

on a yield sign—

summer heat

**American white pelican**

*Pelecanus erythrorhynchos*

Pelicans gather

on the old white concrete dam—

brown water rushing

**Mallard**

*Anas platyrhynchos*

Old man at a pond

sitting on a small stone bench

throwing seeds at ducks

**Great horned owl**

*Bubo virginianus*

Owl orphans

in the enclosure,

sleeping

**Trumpeter swan**

*Cygnus buccinator*

Rustling leaves—

white feathers glide

across the pond

**Canada goose**
*Branta canadensis*

Goose on a knoll,

hissing, on patrol—

no one can pay his toll

**Bufflehead**

*Bucephala albeola*

Corporate koi pond

had some fancy buffleheads—

they left the next day

**Wood duck**

*Aix sponsa*

Swimming under trees,

barely visible wood ducks—

oil-paint feathers

**Barn swallow**

*Hirundo rustica*

Swallows searching

for bugs above the water—

jets flying by

**Baltimore oriole**

*Icterus galbula*

Oriole's belly

looks like orange juice—

my mouth waters

**Yellow-headed blackbird**

*Xanthocephalus xanthocephalus*

Ninety-three,

mid-July near some reeds—

yellow-headed birds

**Bald eagle**

*Haliaeetus leucocephalus*

Between two cliffs,

an eagle swoops—

twenty below

**Northern shoveler**

*Spatula clypeata*

Green, gray, white,

a longer bill than most—

"those ducks are good for hunting"

**Cedar waxwing**

*Bombycilla cedrorum*

Oxbow lakes surrounded by berries

— —

───────────────

and waxwings

**Northern flicker**

*Colaptes auratus*

Dense woods' edge—

a northern flicker

flies in

**American bittern**

*Botaurus lentiginosus*

On the river bank

a statuesque bittern—

disappearing in grass

**American woodcock**

*Scolopax minor*

*Peent*, *flash*, *whistle*—

flying up in circles

just to come back

**Hooded merganser**

*Lophodytes cucullatus*

Hooded mergansers

fly over seven hunters—

they choose not to shoot

**Green heron**

*Butorides virescens*

Pond islet—

heron staring,

waiting for a meal

**Barred owl**

*Strix varia*

Riparian zone—

a barred owl sings

further back

**Great blue heron**

*Ardea herodias*

Slate

feathers

standing up tall

in water—

heron

**Wild turkey**

*Meleagris gallopavo*

Turkeys strutting unaware my dog lurks

**Yellow warbler**

*Setophaga petechia*

Yellow bird

flap-bounding to the

cottonwood

**Peregrine falcon**

*Falco peregrinus*

From the peak

I watch a falcon dive—

the wind picks up

**American barn owl**

*Tyto furcata*

The owl's screech

startles me—

I'm not alone

**Double-crested cormorant**

*Nannopterum auritum*

Flooded dead tree,

adorned

with cormorants

**Belted kingfisher**
*Megaceryle alcyon*

Glacial refuge—

kingfishers

swoop

**Canada jay**

*Perisoreus canadensis*

Our morn camp breakfast

is cooking on the gas stove—

gray jays above us

**Greater sage-grouse**

*Centrocercus urophasianus*

Rolling Wyoming—

sage wilderness and some grouse

pass by on both sides

**Common loon**

*Gavia immer*

Dawn—

a light lake breeze

broken by a loon's yell

**Western meadowlark**

*Sturnella neglecta*

A bird lands

on a pasture's fence post—

it's lonely out here

**Common raven**

*Corvus corax*

A raven

on a roadside tree

watches park visitors

**Common merganser**

*Mergus merganser*

Above the falls,

a single merganser—

autumn mountains

**American dipper**

*Cinclus mexicanus*

Dippers in mountain streams

throw themselves under currents—

sometimes they slip

**Sandhill crane**

*Antigone canadensis*

Driving at dusk,

a large V passes

over our car

**Snowy egret**

*Egretta thula*

Snowy egrets

near the shore—

fading leaves

**American robin**

*Turdus migratorius*

Raining—

depressed at the stoplight—

a spring robin

**American kestrel**

*Falco sparverius*

On the power line,

an American kestrel—

broken-down sedan

**Ruby-throated hummingbird**

*Archilochus colubris*

Buzzing——

iridescent

flash

**Canvasback**

*Aythya valisineria*

Ducks on the water

with deeper colors than most—

I begin to cry

**Black-capped chickadee**

*Poecile atricapillus*

Window feeder—

the cat swats at the chickadee—

it doesn't flinch

**Dark-eyed junco**

*Junco hyemalis*

Little gray birds

under the feeder—

dead of winter

**Northern cardinal**
*Cardinalis cardinalis*

Visitor

to my only winter feeder—

northern cardinal

**White-breasted nuthatch**

*Sitta carolinensis*

Bird

    in

the

  maple

      hopping

face

   down

**Red-bellied woodpecker**

*Melanerpes carolinus*

Woodpecker in the tall maple,

the tapping stops

**Eastern screech owl**

*Megascops asio*

Amidst cicadas

a faint warble in the tree

welcomes the new moon

# Index of artists

**Audubon, John James**

American barn owl, 80

American dipper, 98
(via Robert Havell)

American white pelican, 34
(via Robert Havell)

Belted kingfisher, 84
(etched by William Home Lizars)

Canada goose, 42
(via Robert Havell)

Common grackle, 16

Common merganser, 96
(via Robert Havell)

Double-crested cormorant, 82
(printed by John T. Bowen)

Great horned owl, 38
(etched by William Home Lizars)

Red-bellied woodpecker, 120
(printed by John T. Bowen)

Snowy egret, 102
(etched by William Home Lizars)

**Bierstadt, Albert**

*Landscape*, 124

**Brooks, Allan**

Yellow-headed blackbird, 52

Green heron, 68

**Cabrera, D. A.**

Peregrine falcon, 78

**Edwards, George**

Northern harrier, 26
(engraved by Johann Michael Seligmann)

**Fery, John**

*Glacier Park*, 0

**Fuertes, Louis Agassiz**

Bald eagle, 54

Canvasback, 110

Common nighthawk, 14
(reproduced by Thomas Gilbert Pearson)

Cooper's hawk, 8

Downy woodpecker, 12

Eastern screech owl, 122

Hooded merganser, 66

Northern flicker, 60

Red-tailed hawk, 22

Ring-billed gull, 28

White-faced ibis, 30

Yellow warbler, 76

**Hennessey, Frank**
Cedar waxwing, 58
Ruby-throated hummingbird, 108

**Hines, Robert W.**
White-breasted nuthatch, 118

**Horsfall, Robert Bruce**
Greater sage-grouse, 88
Western meadowlark, 92
Common raven, 94
Dark-eyed junco, 114
American robin, 104

**Kalmbach, Edwin Richard**
American crow, 18
Trumpeter swan, 40
Baltimore oriole, 50
Sandhill crane, 100
American kestrel, 106

**Keulemans, John Gerrard**
Killdeer, 24
Barn swallow, 48
Canada jay, 86

**Koekkoek, Marinus Adrianus (the Younger)**
Mallard, 36
Northern shoveler, 56

**Inman, Henry & Childs, Cephas G.**
American woodcock, 64

**Morris, Beverley Robinson**
Bufflehead, 44
(adapted by Benjamin Fawcett)

**Oudart, Paul Louis**
Turkey vulture, 20

**Prang, Louis**
Red-winged blackbird, 32

**Rich, Walter Herbert**
Wood duck, 46

**Seton, Ernest Thompson**
Barred owl, 70
Great blue heron, 72
Wild turkey, 74
Common loon, 90

**Sheppard, Edwin L.**
Mourning dove, 10

**Thorburn, Archibald**
American bittern, 62

**Unknown**
Northern cardinal, 116

**von Wright brothers**
Black-capped chickadee, 112

www.ingramcontent.com/pod-product-compliance
Lightning Source LLC
Chambersburg PA
CBHW052130030426
42337CB00028B/5096